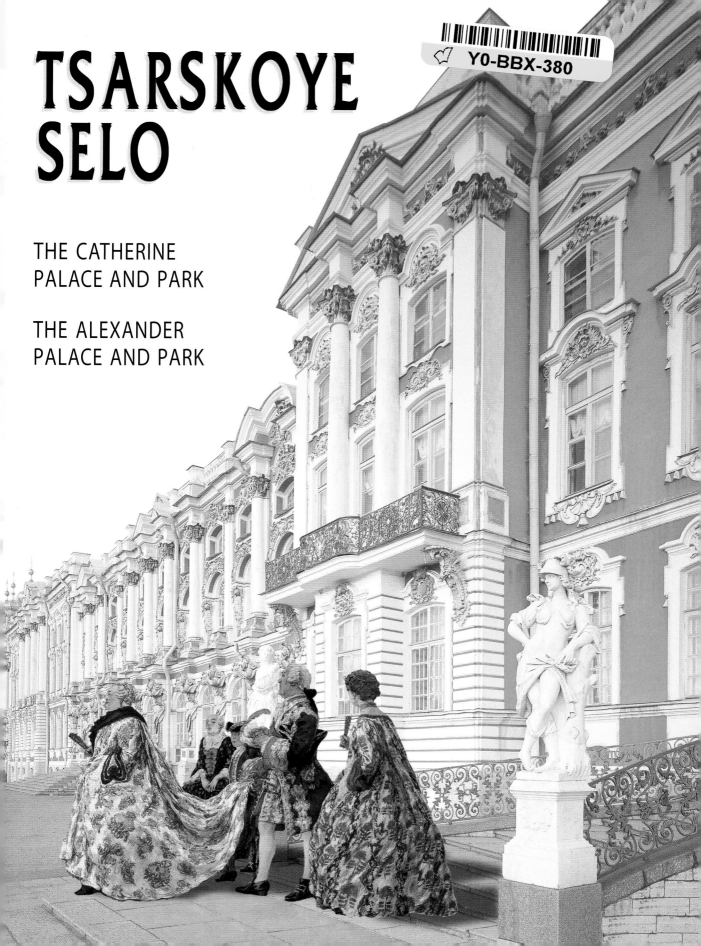

TSARSKOYE SELO

THE CATHERINE PALACE AND PARK

THE ALEXANDER PALACE AND PARK

Text: *Natalia Popova and Abram Raskin*

Translation: *Valery Fateyev*

Design: *Nikolai Kutovoy*

Photographs: *Valentin Baranovsky, Leonid Bogdanov,
Sergei Chistobayev, Vladimir Davydov, Pavel Demidov,
Vladimir Denisov, Alexander Fomichev, Pavel Ivanov,
Alexander Kashnitsky, Vladimir Melnikov, Nikolai Rakhmanov,
Viktor Savik, Georgy Shablovsky, Evgueny Siniaver, Oleg Trubsky,
Vasily Vorontsov*

Editors: *Irina Kharitonova, Irina Lvova*

Computer layout: *Svetlana Bashun*

Colour correction: *Viacheslav Bykovski, Vladimir Kniazev,
Alexander Kondratov, Serguei Ludzski, Alexander Miagkov,
Dmitry Trofimov, Sergei Vyrtosu*

Tsarskoye Selo — the very name of this palace-and-park ensemble provokes a number of happy recollections. In addition to its beautiful parks and architecture, it is also associated with the great age of Russian poetry and the ceremonial glamour of the past autocratic life. In the seventeenth century, there was the Swedish farmstead *Saritsa*, later renamed *Saris hoff*, in this area. The Finnish name of the farmstead was *Saaris moisio* ("a farmstead on the elevation") and its Russianized form was *Sarskaya myza*. After Russia had eventually taken hold of these lands, Sarskaya myza (or Sarskoye Selo) became the property of Alexander Menshikov, and from 1708 to 1724 it was the summer residence of Peter the Great's wife, Yekaterina Alexeyevna (future Catherine I). In 1711, after she was declared "the true Sovereign", the building of a large-scale residence began on the site. Johann Braunstein and Johann Christian Förster were mainly responsible for its construction.

Catherine I bequathed Sarskoye Selo to her daughter, Tsarevna Elizabeth Petrovna. On becoming the Empress in 1741, she, with her innate breadth of nature, did not spare funds for turning the old mansion into a luxurious palace, for building various pavilions and for laying-out gardens. In 1743–51 the Empress's projects for the extension of the suburban residence were carried out by Mikhail Zemtsov, Alexei Kvasov and Savva Chevakinsky. In 1752–56, the work on the estate, by then already renamed Tsarskoye Selo, or the Tsars' Village, was supervised by Bartolomeo Francesco Rastrelli. It was he who gave to the palace and the entire complex that luxurious Baroque appearance which was poetically compared with a "celestial constellation". It was only during the reign of Elizabeth, and through the efforts of Rastrelli, who believed that palaces should be created "for the common glory of Russia", that this residence could rightfully be called — the Tsar's Village.

In 1744, Elizabeth Petrovna commissioned Rastrelli to build "a palace with truly splendid ornaments, fit to be an abode for the ruler of a huge empire". "At first, while the palace was under construction, the ornaments gleamed, and when Empress Elizabeth arrived to view it in the company of her entire court and the foreign ministers, they were all stunned by its splendour, and each of the courtiers rushed to express his amazement" (Mikhail Pyliayev).

A group of actors, under the direction of the son of the Yaroslavl merchant Fiodor Volkov, made its first appearance before a royal audience in the Catherine Palace. Empress Elizabeth, who had heard a great deal about the talents of the young actors, wished to witness them for herself.

1

3

2

Delighted by what she saw, Elizabeth invited Volkov and his associates to Petersburg, and in 1756 she issued a decree on the founding of the Russian professional theatre.

Later on, Empress Catherine II devoted much time and care to the development of the estate and "here her genius and fine taste were revealed". During the reign of Catherine the Great Tsarskoye Selo was further enriched with the works of the architects Antonio Rinaldi, Yury Velten, Vasily Neyelov, Charles Cameron and Giacomo Quarenghi, whose tastes were formed under the influence of ancient architecture.

The Alexander Palace was built by Catherine the Great as a gift to her first and favourite grandson Alexander Pavlovich (the future Alexander I) on the occasion of his wedding to Grand Duchess Elizabeth Alexeyevna, née the Baden Princess Luise-Marie-Augusta. Carrying out the imperial commission, Giacomo Quarenghi created in 1792–96 one of the most perfect landmarks of world architecture the significance of which is not subject to the influence of time. This delightful building is the architectural and aesthetic centrepiece of the Alexander Park. The palace's façades are very simple. They are adorned with colonnade comprising double rows of Corinthian columns.

1. B. Coffre. *Portrait of Peter the Great.*
First quarter of the 18th century

2. I. Adolsky. *Portrait of Empress
Catherine I.* 1726

3. H. Buchgolz. *Portrait of Empress
Elizabeth Petrovna.* 1760s

4. V. Languer. *The Great Pond.
View of the Chesme Column.* 1820.
Watercolour

5. V. Sadovnikov. *The Catherine Palace
as viewed from the main courtyard.*
1840s. Watercolour

6

7 8

9

6. M. Ivanov. *The Great Pond. View of the Chesme Column.*
1790s. Watercolour

7. Anonymous artist. *Emperor Alexander I with the Grand
Dukes Nicholas Pavlovich and Konstantin Pavlovich*

8. V. Borovikovsky. *Catherine the Great on a Stroll
in the Tsarskoye Selo Park*

9. Anonymous artist.
Empress Elizabeth Alexeyevna, Wife of Alexander I

10. H. Vernet. *Knight Tournament in Tsarskoye Selo.
Empress Alexandra Fiodorovna and Emperor Nicholas I
Dressed in Mediaeval Suits.* 1842

11. V. Languer. *The Great Pond. The Cameron Gallery
and the Grotto.* 1820. Engraving

10

11

12

13

14

Catherine the Great personally oversaw the education of Alexander I, Paul's eldest son, and patronised him in a number of ways. The Empress wanted to make him her heir in order to deprive Paul, whom she disliked, of his right to the throne and thus vex her son even from beyond the grave. Although Alexander I almost did not live in the palace on his accession to the throne, this great creation by Quarenghi bears his name.

When Alexander I became Emperor after the assassination of his father, which was committed with Alexander's mute consent, the palace was given to the future tsar, Grand Duke Nicholas. Alexander III also lived there prior to his ascension to the throne, and Nicholas II chose the palace as his permanent residence. The Alexander Palace became the last refuge of the royal family after Nicholas II was deposed in March 1917. From here, he and his family were taken to Tobolsk and then to Ekaterinburg, where they were executed in July 1918.

12. A. Ukhtomsky. *The Bedchamber of the Empress Elizabeth Alexeyevna.* Mid-19th century. Watercolour

13. L. Premazzi. *The Picture Hall.* 1870. Watercolour

14. L. Premazzi. *The Great Hall of the Agate Rooms.* Mid-19th century. Watercolour

15. E. Gau. *The Arabesque Room in the Great Palace of Tsarskoye Selo.* 1850. Watercolour

16. F. H. Barisien. *View of the Great Palace of Tsarskoye Selo.* 1760. Watercolour

17. A. Colbat. *The Third Anteroom in the Great Palace of Tsarskoye Selo.* 1865. Watercolour

15

16

17

20

←

18. Catherine Palace. 1752–56, architect: B.F. Rastrelli

19. Catherine Palace. Detail of the façade

20. Catherine Palace. Moulded decoration of the façade

21, 22. Catherine Palace. Main Porch

21

22

THE CATHERINE PALACE

It is the Catherine Palace the fronts of which ex-
tend for 740 metres, that dominates the entire complex of Tsarskoye Selo. Rastrelli not only completely
altered the dimensions of the latter, but also adorned
them with lavish sculptural designs inside and out.
The palace's external ornaments give a highly accu-
rate impression of the creativeness and imagina-
tion of the architect, who succeeded in endowing the 300 metre long façade with a plastic
expressiveness. No expense was spared on
this building: 100 kilograms of gold alone
were used for the decorations.

23. Catherine Palace.
Palace Church

24. Catherine Palace.
Central part of the garden façade

25. Catherine Palace.
Moulded decoration of the façade

25

26

26. Catherine Palace. Main Staircase

27. Catherine Palace. Main Staircase. Vase.
17th century. Porcelain. China

27

THE MAIN STAIRCASE

The impression of the palace's truly imperial magnificence is enhanced by its interiors, the decor of which reflects the rapidly changing tastes of their crowned owners. This change can be observed in the design of the imperial apartments where Baroque luxury neighbours with Classical elegance.

The famous marble Main Staircase by Hippolyto Monighetti, is striking for the monumental character of its design. The staircase with two tiers of windows overlooking the Catherine and Alexander Parks occupies a special place in the composition of the Catherine Palace. It is from this interior that the overall conception of the palace and park ensemble can be most clearly perceived.

The Main Staircase is designed in the style that makes it comparable to Rastrelli's interiors. The rocaille moulded ornamentation of the walls and ceilings, the paintings by Italian painters of the seventeenth and eighteenth centuries adorning the ceiling, the pieces of marble sculpture (*Sleeping Cupid* and *Awakening Cupid*) on the landings, the Japanese and Chinese porcelain on the wall consoles, all makes this palatial staircase particularly impressive.

28, 29. Catherine Palace. Main Staircase. Upper landing

30. Catherine Palace. Great Hall.
Detail of the interior

31. Catherine Palace. Great Hall

32. Catherine Palace. Great Hall.
Detail of the ceiling painting

31

THE GREAT HALL

The Great Hall (or the Ballroom) is a true master-piece of the decorative genius of Bartolomeo Francesco Rastrelli. This is one of the largest palatial halls created by this outstanding architect in St Petersburg and its environs in the 1750s.

The hall's area is 846 square metres (it is seventeen metres wide and forty-seven metres long). Bright and airy, the room seems even larger than it actually is because of the many mirrors, the abundance of gilding and, in particular, the spectacular painted ceiling, which creates an illusion of endless space.

Rastrelli wanted the room to be perceived as an integral whole, so he concealed the stoves necessary to heat this huge hall behind false windows with mirrored glass. The impression of its great expanse is still further enhanced thanks to the illusion of space created by the two tiers of windows.

The main element in the decoration of the Great Hall is gilded carving. The endless figures and half-figures — putti and "seated ladies", interlacing ornaments, whimsical cartouches and rocailles strike us by their exceedingly imaginative and still realistic treatment. During the restoration of the Great Hall some parts of the carved work were restored and some

others were recreated from similar examples in accordance with the techniques of woodwork employed in the eighteenth century.

The grandiose ceiling painting *The Triumph of Russia* and the fanciful pattern of the inlaid parquetry enhance the decorative effect of the Great Hall. The elaborate pictorial composition of *The Triumph of Russia* in the centre of the ceiling consists of three pictures executed by Giuseppe Valeriani, an eminent master of decorative painting. The parquet floor with star-shaped diverging rays made after Rastrelli's sketch from the woods available in Russia — light and tinted oak, maple and walnut — was restored.

33. Catherine Palace. Great Hall. View of the east wall

The piers between the windows are covered with mirrors in gilded carved frames. A sense of lightness is increased by the mirrors imitating windows on the butt-end walls and set in the piers and on the doors.

34. Catherine Palace. Great Hall. Details of the interior

35. Catherine Palace. Great Hall. Door decoration

Nevertheless the predominant decorative element of the interior is gilded carving. Countless figures and half-figures, ornamental interlaces, cartouches and rocailles produce an indelible impression on visitors by their fantastic ingenuity and mastery of their execution.

THE DINING ROOM FOR CAVALIERS-IN-ATTENDANCE

Along with majestic ceremonies the palace was the venue of more intimate receptions to which only guests belonging to a narrow circle were invited. Next to the Great Hall is the Dining Room for Cavaliers-in-Attendance where parties of this sort were held. This Dining Room is remarkable for its golden decor shining in numerous mirrors as well as for the painted insets of hunting scenes in round frames over the mirrors as well as for the fine table appointments and decoration. It is interesting that in the middle of the eighteenth century the tables were not standing here permanently but were brought in only for dinners.

The ceiling painting by an anonymous Russian painter of the mid-eighteenth century is devoted to a subject from ancient Greek mythology. It features Helios, the sun god, and Eos, the goddess of the dawn, surrounded by the allegories of seasons.

36. Catherine Palace.
Dining Room for Cavaliers-in-Attendance. Tiled stove

37, 38. Catherine Palace.
Dining Room for Cavaliers-in-Attendance

THE PORTRAIT HALL
THE WHITE DINING ROOM

Symmetrically to the Dining Room for Cavaliers-in-Attendance, to the north of the Main Staircase, is the White Dining Room, followed by the Portrait Hall showing large representative portraits of the Empresses Catherine I and Elizabeth. In the eighteenth century, the age of amusements and festivities, a great significance was attached to the laying and decoration of tables. The feasts held in the White Dining Room were especially sumptuous. The table, shaped like the *E* monogram, was skilfully draped by a snow-white cloth adorned with garlands of flowers. It was set with the so-called Her Majesty's Own Service produced at the celebrated Fiodor Gardner Porcelain Factory that rivalled the Imperial Factory in terms of the quality of its articles. The walls of the Dining Room are embellished with paintings by the court artist Johann Friedrich Grooth featuring hunting scenes.

39. Catherine Palace. Portrait Hall

40– 42. Catherine Palace. White Dining Room

THE CRIMSON AND GREEN PILASTER DRAWING ROOMS

The Golden Suite unites into a single whole a series of ornate interiors running along the first floor of the Catherine Palace. The walls and window surrounds in these departments are trimmed with gilded carvings forming rocaille ornamental and figure compositions; the ceiling is embellished with stuccowork shining with gold and paintings; the floor is decorated with inlaid parquetry. The white damask, which is used to upholster the walls of the rooms, has been woven on special looms after eighteenth-century original examples. All the rooms of this state enfilade contain stoves with niches and fancy-shaped cornices decorated with cobalt painting in imitation of tiles.

The Crimson and Green Pilaster Drawing Rooms following the White State Dining Room have an unusual and impressive appearance. They owe much

43. Catherine Palace. Green Pilaster Drawing Room.
Detail of the upholstery

44. Catherine Palace. Picture Hall.
Detail of the decor

45. Catherine Palace. Perspective view of the suite
of state rooms (known as the Golden Enfilade)

46. Catherine Palace.
Green Pilaster Drawing Room

47. Catherine Palace.
Green Pilaster Drawing Room.
Ceiling painting

of their unusual look to the pilasters rhythmically articulating the walls. These are made of glass with brightly coloured foil put under it, so that the texture of the foil is reminiscent of a play of gems. Framed by gilded carving, these pilasters look highly ornate. The Crimson and Green Drawing Rooms are decorated with ceiling paintings. In the eighteenth century they had no special designation.

Nowadays the exhibition displayed in these rooms emphasizes its playing character. The card table in the centre of the room bears China-made chess carved in ivory, with mother-of-pearl insets.

An indispensable attribute in all the interiors of the Catherine Palace created by Rastrelli was a tall hexagonal stove faced with tiles painted in cobalt blue. Such stoves can be seen in the Crimson and Green Pilaster Drawing Rooms, too.

48. Catherine Palace. Crimson Pilaster Drawing Room

49

50

THE AMBER ROOM

Powerful baroc forms determine the plastic expressiveness of the palace endowing it with a truly regal majesty. This impression is enhanced by the interiors of the palace the decor of which reflects the swiftly changing tastes of the crowned owners. They are recorded in the decorative styles of the rooms and halls.

A veritable gem of the Catherine Palace was the Amber Study which is justly ranked by connoisseurs among "treasures of the world".

In 1701–09 Gottfried Wolfram, Gottfried Turau and Ernst Schacht produced, after a design by Andreas Schlüter, the inlaid amber panels which in 1717 were sent by the Prussian king, Frederick William I, to Peter the Great as a gift for the decoration of the Study in his Winter Palace at St Petersburg. In 1755 Rastrelli designed the Amber Room in the Catherine Palace enriching the panels with Florentine mosaics and sculpture. The unpanelled area of the walls was skilfully decorated with mirrors, murals and gilded wood-carving.

Anyone who ever saw the Amber Room was enchanted by it. One French author once wrote that: "The eye, unused to seeing amber in such quantities,

49, 53. Catherine Palace. Amber Room

50. Catherine Palace. Amber Room.
Detail of the amber panel

51, 52. Catherine Palace. Amber Room.
Details of the interior decor

51

52

54. Catherine Palace. Amber Room. Frederick I's coat of arms. Amber. Detail of the lower frieze decor

55. Catherine Palace. Amber Room. Detail of the interior

58

56. Catherine Palace. Amber Room.
Clock decorated with porcelain flowers.
Mid-18th century. Bronze, porcelain.
Workshop of G. Cosar, France

57. Catherine Palace. Amber Room
Detail of the interior decor

58. Catherine Palace. Amber Room

59. Catherine Palace. Amber Room.
Casket. 1705. Amber, wood, metal.
By G. Turau, Germany

59

is captivated and blinded by the wealth and warmth of the tones, which encompass every shade of yellow, from dusky topaz to bright lemon…"

During the Second World War, almost all amber objects were removed to Novosibirsk, but the panels of the Amber Room were looted by the Nazi soldiers. The current exhibition is comprised of the works that were saved or restored. The mosaics lining the walls are being recreated by contemporary craftsmen. Fortunately, the room has nowadays completely regained its former splendour.

THE PICTURE HALL

The Picture Hall, an interior the decor of which is largely devoted to painting, is characteristic of the first half of the eighteenth century. The powerful decorative effect created by tapestry-like hanging of the canvases combines here with the image of a picture gallery, an indispensable attribute in the home of an enlightened aristocrat during that period.

Rastrelli completely covered the longitudinal walls with 130 paintings by Luca Giordano, Emmanuel de Witte, Adriaen van Ostade, David Teniers and other eminent Western European artists of the seventeenth and eighteenth centuries. Two paintings, *The Battle of Poltava* and *The Battle of Lesnaya*, were commissioned by Peter the Great from the French painter Pierre Denis Martin.

60. Catherine Palace. Picture Hall

61. Catherine Palace. Picture Hall. Detail of the inlaid parquet floor

62. Catherine Palace. Picture Hall. Door decoration

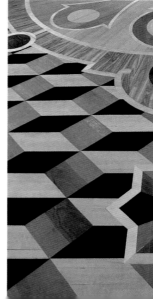

THE GREEN DINING ROOM

The Green Dining Room, decorated after drawings by Cameron, represents a version of the subtle interpretation of ancient motifs in the Russian interiors of the 1780s. Cameron freely improvised on the subject of ancient Roman decorative motifs. He attained the harmony of his artistic solution primarily by the use of plastic elements. The moulded details are arranged against the light green background of the walls with a thorough calculation. The main field is enlivened by a stylized representation of garden gates with medallions and moulded figures of youths and girls, seemingly supporting bas-reliefs with scenes of playing Cupids. The crowning element of the wall composition are arc-shaped twigs of vine. The delicate tracery of details and the jeweller's modelling of sculptural forms executed by Ivan Martos after Cameron's drawings lend the Green Dining Room that sense of elegance which dominates the living apartments of the Catherine Palace.

63–65. Catherine Palace. Green Dining Room

66. Catherine Palace. Green Dining Room.
Fireplace. 1780s. Designed by Ch. Cameron

63

64   65

67

THE BLUE DRAWING ROOM

The Blue Drawing Room, the central apartment of the north section of the palace, is one of the most remarkable interiors in the palace created by Cameron in the 1780s. Notable features of this interior are the silk upholstery of its walls adorned with a printed pattern, the artistic paintings of the ceilings and doors as well as the inlaid parquet floor. In all this majestic spectacle free improvisations of motifs borrowed from ancient art can be traced. Set into the moulded frieze with a gilded relief ornament are painted medallions featuring ancient

69

images. The ceiling of the Blue Drawing Room is embellished with decorative painting based on semi-circles, rectangles and squares. Painted within the geometrical figures are mythological scenes and characters. The rich design of the inlaid parquet floor matches the elaborate compositional forms of the painted ceiling. Cameron especially loved to use unusual combinations of painting, gilding, decorative fabrics and items of furniture in his interiors. In the Blue Drawing Room, for example, pale blue silk with a flower print serves as a delightful backdrop for the austere Classical forms of the furniture

and mirrors. The standard lamps made of blue glass and positioned in the corners of the room make a delightful addition to its decorative fittings. In Cameron's day, fireplaces for heating the vast rooms first appeared in the palace chambers and were constructed precisely according to his designs.

67, 69. Catherine Palace. Blue Drawing Room

68. Catherine Palace. Blue Drawing Room. Clock: *Bacchus*. 18th century. Gilded bronze. France

68

41

70. Catherine Palace.
Chinese Blue Drawing Room.
Detail of the upholstery

71. Catherine Palace.
Decorative statuettes: *Chinese Man*
and *Chinese Woman*. Porcelain. China

72

THE CHINESE BLUE DRAWING ROOM

The Chinese Blue Drawing Room is otherwise known as the Main Study. The silks and porcelain fittings used in the decor of this chamber were brought to Russia in the mid-eighteenth century when trade links with China began to develop. Its walls are lined from top to bottom with blue silk which is embellished with stylized scenes of "Chinese life" painted in vari-coloured inks.

It is remarkable that Cameron, a convinced Classicist, combined the *chinoiserie* upholstery of the walls with ancient motifs of the ceiling painting, which lent the interior an air of artistic originality. The silk used for lining the walls in the reign of Catherine the Great was brought from China, but it was destroyed during the Second World War. The lost fabrics were recreated by restorers on the basis of a surviving sample.

72, 73. Catherine Palace. Chinese Blue Drawing Room

73

43

THE BEDROOM

During the reign of Catherine the Great, new interiors appeared in the palace, associated with Cameron. The use of subtly adapted forms derived from Greco-Roman decor is characteristic of the works of this outstanding master of Classicism. Catherine the Great commissioned Cameron the designing of the heir's apartments, and Cameron brilliantly coped with the task.

The Bedroom of Maria Fiodorovna is one of the most spectacular interiors created by Cameron in the Catherine Palace. This is the largest of Paul I and Maria Fiodorovna's private rooms. The architectural image of this room combined the intimate character of a private apartment with the luxury of a state room. Elegant alcoves and refined decorations lend the chamber a special charm. Cameron used for the decor of the Bedroom moulded wall panels executed by Ivan Martos, which allegorically personified joy and happiness of family life.

The most prominent feature of the Bedroom are slender faience columns of the alcove. Lavishly ornamented and emphasized by gilded strips and flutes, they are entwined with garlands. Arranged with a subtle sense of rhythm, the stucco frieze against the pale green walls, and the delicately gilded mouldings are all reminiscent of the features of the famous Pompeiian villas' murals.

74. Catherine Palace. Bedchamber

75. Catherine Palace. Bedchamber. Door decoration

76. Catherine Palace. Bedchamber.
Cupid. Second half of the 18th century, sculptor: N. Gillee

75

THE CHOIR ANTEROOM

The Choir Anteroom is an interior in the northern half of the palace that Empress Catherine allotted to Grand Duke Pavel Petrovich, the heir to the throne, and his wife, Grand Duchess Maria Fiodorovna. The Choir Anteroom owes its name to its location near the choir of the home church. As is known, Catherine invited the Scottish architect Charles Cameron to design the interior. However, the stylistic elements typical of this outstanding exponent of Classicism can hardly be discerned in the decor of the Choir Anteroom, because it has been repeatedly altered.

The distinctive feature of this interior is the trimming of its walls with silk bearing woven varicoloured depictions of swans and pheasants. The fabric was produced by Russian weavers from a sketch made in France for the Lyons Factory. The silk is authentic and therefore very rare — during the war the staff members succeeded to evacuate it to the hinterland.

The gilded eighteenth-century set of furniture installed in the Choir Anteroom was made after a drawing by Rastrelli and later upholstered with a nineteenth-century silk. The decor of the Choir Anteroom lends to this interior, modest in dimensions, the majesty of a true state room.

77. Catherine Palace. Choir Anteroom. Detail of the upholstery

78. Catherine Palace. Choir Anteroom

79. Catherine Palace. White Dining Room. Vase (incense burner). 18th century. Porcelain. Meissen, Germany

79

THE STATE (MARBLE) STUDY
THE CHURCH OF THE RESURRECTION
THE CHURCH ANTEROOM

Besides state rooms, drawing rooms and living quarters, Bartolomeo Francesco Rastrelli incorporated a chapel into his designs for the palace. It became known as the Church of the Resurrection and stood in the east wing of the building. The church was built in 1745–48 by Rastrelli with a contribution by Alexei Kvasov and Savva Chevakinsky. Grand Duke Nikolai Pavlovich was baptized here. It was also in this palatial church that the coffin with the body of Emperor Alexander I who died at Taganrog was installed.

People used to wait for the beginning of the service in the spacious, richly decorated Church Anteroom designed by Vasily Stasov in the 1840s. This interior is situated between the Church and the vestibule of the ground floor.

The State or Marble Study of Emperor Alexander I, created in 1817, was intended for important official receptions. Alexander I liked to sit at the desk in this room, working late into the quiet Tsarskoye Selo evenings. The malachite ink-stand and bronze candlesticks on the desk belonged to the Emperor himself. The room was designed

80. Catherine Palace. Church Anteroom

81. Catherine Palace. Church of the Resurrection. Interior

82. Catherine Palace. State (Marble) Study

by Vasily Stasov, whose work completes the evolution of Russian Classicism. So he adorned the Study in the Empire style. The two Ionic columns separate a niche from the main, rectangular volume of the Study. The decor of the frieze and dome of the niche includes Classical motifs — depictions of Roman panoply and laurel wreaths. The walnut furniture set made by the famous St Petersburg companies, those of F. Grosset and Heinrich Gambs after a sketch by Stasov has been restored to its former appearance.

83. Catherine Palace. Central part
of the façade

84. Hermitage alley
seen from the Catherine Palace

85. Catherine Palace.
Decorative sculpture near the Main Porch

84

THE CATHERINE PARK

86. The façade of the Catherine Palace seen from the pond

87. Catherine Park. Cameron Gallery. 1784–87, architect: Ch. Cameron

88. Catherine Park. Cameron Ramp. Decorative vase. 1828. Bronze. Designed by V. Stasov

89. Catherine Park. Old Garden. Parterre

90. Catherine Park. Cameron Gallery. Main Staircase

In 1728, Tsarskoye Selo became the property of Elizabeth Petrovna following a decree issued by Peter the Great. Before ascending to the throne, she often came here to hunt and oversee the cultivation of the orchards on the estate. When Empress Elizabeth decided to create a little Versailles in Tsarskoye Selo, she accorded Bartolomeo Francesco Rastrelli complete artistic freedom. He remodelled the main features of the park and palace ensemble for Elizabeth, although they are historically known as the Catherine Park and Catherine Palace respectively.

Rastrelli perfected the regular park that had been planned earlier, stretching out from the east façade of the Catherine Palace. From water, trees, marble and stone he produced a true ode to the eighteenth century. As if by magic, he conjured up mirror ponds, parterre flowerbeds and intricate mazes in which marble sculptures created by Italians charm us with their sensual beauty. The attractive arrangement of alleys laid out in front of the Catherine Palace was ideally suited to unhurried strolls and ceremonial processions. The architect included into his composition two garden pavilions: the Hermitage and the Grotto.

91

92

The oldest part of the Catherine Park is the garden, which stretches out before the east façade of the Catherine Palace. Its avenues are lined with marble sculptures. Only a small number of the statues and busts that were to be found here in the eighteenth and nineteenth centuries have survived to this day. Several of them bear inscriptions. The names of masters of the Venetian school at the turn of the eighteenth century — Pietro Baratta, Antonio Tarsia and Giovanni Bonazza — are to be seen on the pedestals. Works by these sculptors also

91. Catherine Park. Old Garden.
Decorative sculptures. 17th–18th century

92. Catherine Park.
View of the Cameron Gallery from the park

93. Catherine Park. Cameron Ramp. 1792–94,
architect: Ch. Cameron

94. Catherine Park. Cameron Gallery.
View of the colonnade

93

94

95

95. Catherine Park. Agate Rooms. Great Hall

96. E.M. Falconet. *Cupid Menacing with His Finger.* 1758

97. Catherine Park. Agate Rooms from the Hanging Garden. 1784–87, architect: Ch. Cameron

98. Catherine Park. Agate Rooms. Agate Study. Ceiling painting

96

grace the Summer Garden in Petersburg. It was Baratta who created one of the best statues in the garden, the representation of Galatea. This small statue was conceived as the centrepiece of a fountain.

In the 1770s–'80s, buildings that now constitute stylish monuments to Russian Classicism were also erected in the Catherine Park. Catherine the Great once described the work of Charles Cameron in one of her letters: "Now I have got my hands on the master Cameron, a Scotsman by birth, a Jacobin by profession and a great draughtsman, who is full of knowledge of the ancients and is renowned for his book on ancient bathhouses. Here in Tsarskoye Selo we are creating a terraced garden with bathhouses below and a gallery above. It will be charming!" It was not the interiors that brought Cameron the fame he deserved, but the splendid architectural edifices that he built, of which there are several in Tsarskoye Selo. The largest and most illustrious of these is the Cameron Gallery, named after its designer.

The Gallery and the adjoining Agate Rooms, Cold Bath, Hanging Garden and Ramp make up a harmonious "Greco-Roman rhapsody". Indeed, this architectural composition, which comprises several buildings created to serve a variety of functions, is inspiring for its grandeur, originality and the boldness of its design.

The Cameron Gallery created by Cameron, an outstanding interpreter of ancient motifs, is called an architectural "poem" in the spirit of Classicism. Pushkin recalls it a "huge hall" soaring towards clouds and dominating the Catherine Gardens. The Cameron Gallery, intended for meditation, promenades, social intercourse and contemplation of the splendid landscape that stretches out on all sides, plays an important part in the ensemble. The architect chose a truly appropriate spot for it on the slope of the hill leading down to the Great Pond. The ground floor of the Gallery is made of massive stone blocks. Here were the living quarters for courtiers. The bright, glass-faced hall on the first floor, surrounded on all sides by a colonnade, seems still lighter and airier in comparison to the solid ground floor. The magnificent outer staircase with its elegantly curving flight of steps is a wonderful architectural creation in its own right. The Gallery is decorated with 54 busts of philosophers, poets, emperors, military leaders, gods and heroes of antiquity. The only contemporary of Cameron's whose likeness is included in this series is Mikhail Lomonosov.

The Ramp installed by Cameron serves as an organic link between the architectural ensemble and the surrounding landscaped gardens. It also represents one of Cameron's artistic triumphs. The architect

99, 100. Catherine Park. Cameron Ramp. Keystone

101. Catherine Park in winter. View of the Cameron Gallery

102. Catherine Park. Cameron Ramp. 1792–94, architect: Ch. Cameron

103. Catherine Park. Cameron Gallery. *Hercules*. 1786. Copy from an antique original. Cast after the model of F. Gordeyev

99

100

101

102

103

104

105

107

106

treated it in the manner of ancient cyclopean structures like aqueducts, open waterways of Ancient Rome. The decor of the walls is eye-catching: enormous masks cut from local limestone adorn the keystones of the arches. Amongst the heroes of ancient mythology to be seen here are Mercury, Pan, Silenus, Neptune and others. The powerful, gradually descending arches divided by semicircular supports-columns bear the gently sloping descent which is linked to the Ramp Avenue. The composition of the Ramp was completed with bronze statues in 1794. Later, by order of Paul I, they were moved to Pavlovsk, and in 1828 decorative wrought iron bowls reminiscent of ancient lamps were installed to replace them (they are attributed to Stasov).

104. Catherine Park. Private Garden. Decorative vase

105. Catherine Park.
Agate Rooms (Cold Baths). View from the palace

106. Catherine Park. Cameron Gallery. Hanging Garden. *Venus Callipygos*. 19th century. Marble. Copy from an antique original

107. Catherine Park. Private Garden. Alley with a fountain

108. Catherine Park.
Private Garden. *Nymph*. 1860s, sculptor: P. Zabello

109. Catherine Park. Agate Rooms (Cold Baths).
Decorative sculpture

110. Catherine Park. Private Garden.
Lion. Late 19th century. Marble

108

109   110

111. Catherine Park.
Upper Bath Pavilion.
Ceiling painting and murals
(copies of the paintings
of the Neron Domus Aureus).
Mid-19th century.
By A. Belsky according
the watercolours
of F. Smuglevich

112, 113. Catherine Park.
Upper Bath Pavilion.
1777–79, architect: I. Neyelov

114. Catherine Park.
Upper Bath Pavilion.
Detail of the interior

111

The Ramp forms an effective perspective along the middle axis and produces an impression of a complex of triumphal arches from the side.

In 1780–87 Charles Cameron erected the building of the Cold Baths as a single ensemble with the Gallery. The volume and façades of the Cold Baths appear from the side of the gallery as a small pavilion, but from the side of the park it looks like a massive structure. The heavily rusticated fronts of the Cold Baths are decorated with bronze and stone statues. The two-storey building is angled towards the sun just as Roman thermal baths were. On the lower floor are the Cold Baths for which Cameron devised a special plumbing system. The interiors of the upper floor are called the Agate Rooms. They are faced with plaques of coloured stone, mainly marble and jasper of various types and shades. The noble colours of natural stones determine the unique designs of the Amber, Agate and Small Studies, Great Oval Hall, staircase, testifying to the exclusive taste of the architect, sculptors and stone carvers who created this unique ensemble.

116

"Travelling to Tsarskoye with a small retinue, Catherine divided her time between affairs of state and all manner of amusements. Every day she would take a walk in the park in the company of the knights and maids of the court… Of all the country residences, Catherine's favourite was Tsarskoye Selo. From 1763 onwards, with the exception of 2 or 3 years, she lived in Tsarskoye Selo in spring and spent practically all summer here, leaving in the autumn when the weather grew cold. It is here that she celebrated almost every one of her birthdays, and from here that she set out on her ceremonial journey to Petersburg on 28 June 1763 after the coronation in Moscow" (Sergei Vilchkovsky).

Besides the palace and the Cameron Gallery, the Catherine Park contains a number of small pavilions, which serve various purposes. Often located on the shores of a pond or lake, they are magically reflected in the still surface of the waters.

Rastrelli endowed the Hermitage Pavilion with such a decorative majesty that it began to resemble a miniature palace. With her insatiable taste for novel amusements, Elizabeth was par-

ticularly fond of dining with her courtiers in this pavilion. Traditionally, the lower storey of the Hermitage had mechanisms which were used to lift laid tables for meals held in the Central Hall of the upper floor. As a rule the procedure began in the very heat of a ball. The floors would suddenly open and exquisite dishes would appear from below to the guests' pleasant surprise.

The Grotto Pavilion or Morning Room built by Rastrelli on the bank of the Great Pond was used for recreation during boating parties. The pavilion's location and designation determined its fairy-tale moulded decor with sea monsters, dolphins and sea-shells. The Grotto blends beautifully

115. Catherine Park. Hermitage Pavilion. Ceiling painting of the Central Hall

116. Catherine Park. Granite Terrace. 1809–10, architect: L. Rusca

117. Catherine Park. Hermitage Pavilion. 1749–54, architect: B. F. Rastrelli

119

120

121

122

with the panorama of the Great Pond. It is a characteristic example of the small architectural structures that adorn the horizons of the park at Tsarskoye Selo. Unlike the emphatically decorative pavilions in the Baroque style, Classicist architects lent to garden structures geometrically clear-cut shapes accentuated by relief insets. Such is the Upper Bath Pavilion built in the 1770s by the architect Ilya Neyelov.

In 1772–74, the architect Vasily Neyelov erected a remarkable bridge over the Great Pond. It was initially

118. Catherine Park. Granite Terrace.
Statues – copies from antique originals. 1851.
By J. Hamburger

119, 120. Catherine Park.
Busts – allegories of the seasons of the year.
Early 18th century. Marble. Venice

121. Catherine Park. Granite Terrace. *Nymph*. 1851.
Copy from an antique original. By J. Hamburger

122. Catherine Park. Parterre of the Granite Terrace.
Venus and Cupid. 1851. Copy from an antique original.
By J. Hamburger

123

124

125

referred to as the Siberian Marble Gallery, since its component parts were prepared in Ekaterinburg from marble mined in the Urals and delivered to Tsarskoye Selo, where they were assembled over a period of two years. The dark water of the pond reflects and replicates the precise arrangement of the columns. It subsequently came to be known as the Palladian Bridge in honour of the famous Italian architect and theoretician, Andrea Palladio.

Under Catherine the Great, the vast park with an area of 100.5 hectares became a "pantheon of Russian greatness". The unique ensemble of monuments,

123. The Great Pond as viewed from the Cameron Gallery

124. Catherine Park. Grotto Pavilion (Morning Room). 1749–61, architect: B. F. Rastrelli

125. Catherine Park. Palladian Bridge (Siberian Marble Gallery). 1772–74, architect: V. Neyelov

126. Catherine Park. View of the Grotto Pavilion

128

which includes the Chesme Column and the Column of Morea, the Kagul Obelisk and the Crimean Column, commemorates the Turkish campaigns of the 1760s and '70s, the crowning glory of the Russian forces.

The most famous monument to Catherine the Great, the Chesme Rostral Column, soars on a small island of the Great Pond. It was erected to a design by Antonio Rinaldi in 1774–76 to commemorate the victory of the Russian squadron over the Turkish fleet in Chesme Bay in the Aegean Sea in 1770.

The landscaped section of the Catherine Park is situated around the Great Pond. A number of unique park pavilions are connected with it, among which

129

127. Catherine Park.
Bird's-eye view of the Great Pond

128. Catherine Park. Chesme (Orlov) Column.
1774–76, architect: A. Rinaldi

129. Catherine Park. Granite landing-stage
on the bank of the Great Pond

130

131

the Turkish Bath reminiscent of a miniature mosque. It was designed by Hippolyto Monighetti in 1850–52. Built in honour of Russia's victory over the Turks in the war of 1828–29 the pavilion stands on the southwest shore of the pond. Having given his brainchild the external appearance of a mosque with three-tiered minarets, the architect then embellished the interior with genuine articles of Eastern applied art, namely marble slabs taken from fountains and carved with verses in Arabic.

From the 1770s onwards, a preoccupation with "historical" styles such as the Gothic and, in particular, the Oriental "Turkic" and "Chinoiserie" styles, became apparent in the architecture within the gardens. On the shore of the Great Pond, for example, the Admiralty ensemble, consisting of three buildings, was created. The name is derived from the fact that the central structure

130, 132. Catherine Park. Admiralty ("Holland").
1773–77, architect: V. Neyelov

131. Catherine Park. Turkish Bath.
1850–52, architect: H. Monighetti

was used as a boathouse. Its round turret and the arrow slits cut into the brick walls are a testimony to the English Gothic style.

Tsarskoye Selo is not simply dear to Russians because it was one of the imperial country residences for many years. This place is also inseparably linked to the name of the great Russian poet Alexander Pushkin, who studied at the Lyceum (now a branch of the Pushkin Museum) and continued to visit the village at various times throughout his life. Even people who have not been to Tsarskoye Selo can clearly picture its various features and get a feel for their charms when reading the poet's verses. It seems that the writer extols every inch of the park, including the renowned *Milkmaid Fountain, or the Girl with a Pitcher* (1816, sculptor Pavel Sokolov), which was built over the only natural spring in the park. The fountain later on has been celebrated by poets. It is covered by a granite boulder crowned with the bronze figure of a young girl crying over the broken pitcher.

Tsarskoye Selo, which Pushkin associated in his verses with the idea of homeland, became the holy land of Russian poetry for subsequent generations. There are many buildings in Tsarskoye Selo connected with Pushkin's life — the house of Ludwig Wilhelm

134

133. Catherine Park. Kagul Obelisk.
1771–72, architect: A. Rinaldi

134. Catherine Park. Metal Bridge.
1784, architect: G. Quarenghi

135. Catherine Park. Fountain: *The Milkmaid,
or the Girl with a Pitcher*. 1816, sculptor: P. Sokolov

133

Tepper de Ferguson, a music teacher in the Lyceum, and the mansion of Vasily Malinovsky and Yegor Engelgardt, its first directors, the house of the writer and historian Nikolai Karamzin, and the famous Kitayeva's *dacha* which now houses a Pushkin museum. The poet lived at the *dacha* together with his young wife Natalia Goncharova in 1831.

It is the Lyceum that evokes especially vivid associations connected with the poet's youth spent at Tsarskoye Selo. In 1811 the former palatial wing, linked in 1789–91 with the Great Palace by a gallery, was given to the newly founded privileged educational establishment named the Lyceum. Here Alexander Pushkin studied between 1811 and 1817. Pushkin devoted to the Lyceum and Tsarskoye Selo, where "the Muse appeared" to him for the first time, a number of beautiful verses.

On 8 January 1815 in the Assembly Hall of the Lyceum, one of the most important events in the life of Pushkin and the history of Russian poetry took place. Eminent guests, including the outstanding eighteenth-century Russian poet Gavriil Derzhavin, were invited to attend the examinations at the Lyceum, during which the young Pushkin read a poem that he had composed specially for the occasion, entitled

136. Catherine Park.
Ruin Tower. 1771–73,
architect: A. Rinaldi

137. Catherine Park.
Metal Bridge. 1784,
architect: G. Quarenghi

138. Catherine Park.
Private Garden.
View of the pergola

139. Catherine Park.
View of the Great Pond
from the Cameron Gallery

138

139

"Recollections of Tsarskoye Selo". Many years later the poet wrote: "I only saw Derzhavin once, but I will never forget it… He dozed right up until the Russian literature examination, at which point he was completely transformed… At last, my name was called… I cannot describe the state I was in: when I got to the part where I refer to Derzhavin, my voice turned into an adolescent squeak and my heart began to pound with intoxicating delight… I do not recall how I finished the recital; I do not remember where I ran off to. Derzhavin was enraptured, he wanted to embrace me. They looked for me, but they could not find me." That is how Pushkin won his first poetic acclaim. He was fifteen years old.

To commemorate the Lyceum years of Pushkin in honour of the centenary of the poet's birth, on 2 May 1899 a monument to the poet was laid down in the Lyceum garden. It was cast of bronze after a model by the sculptor Robert Bach and opened a year later. A young man, his school uniform unbuttoned and his cap set aside, sits day-dreaming on an old park bench. The inhabitants of Tsarskoye Selo collected funds for the creation of the monument which has recorded for ever their love for the poetic genius of Russia.

143

144

140. Statue of Pushkin in the garden of the Lyceum. 1900, sculptor: R. Bach

141. Catherine Palace church and the Lyceum

142. Lyceum. Great Hall. 1811, architect: V. Stasov

143. I. Repin. *Pushkin at the Lyceum Examination in Tsarskoye Selo on 8 January 1815.* 1911

144. Lyceum. Pushkin's room

145

The Golden Gate decorates the main entrance to the Catherine Palace. Behind it, in keeping with the tradition of eighteenth-century architecture, is the formal courtyard arranged in front of the main west façade of the palace adorned with semicircular service wings. In 1752–56 Rastrelli stylistically united the service blocks with the Baroque courtyard. Put up in the gaps between them were fences and gates with pylons. The graphic silhouette of the forged frame is enhanced and completed by a variety of elaborate gilded scrolls, garlands, sea-shells, feathers and stars.

The main gate is crowned with the Imperial coat of arms, the gilded double-headed eagle, which emphasizes the designation of Tsarskoye Selo as a royal residence.

145, 147. Railings of the gate of the Catherine Palace

146. Catherine Palace. Cupolas of the palace church

148. View of the main gate and courtyard

146

147

148

149

THE ALEXANDER PALACE
THE ALEXANDER PARK

Beyond the bounds of the main estate at Tsarskoye Selo lies another famous park. The Alexander Park was laid in the early nineteenth century and combines regular gardens and landscaped features. The design of the palace blends subtly with the surrounding landscape so that the building becomes an integral part of the natural setting rather than the dominant feature. The Alexander Palace largely owes its rare magnificence to the double colonnade uniting the extending parts of the north front, with a happily found rhythm of the "movement" of slender shafts crowned by the capitals of the Corinthian order.

During the reign of Nicholas I it became the favourite residence of the Emperor's family who lived in Alexander Palace from the early spring till the end of May and after a short stay at Krasnoye Selo during manoeuvres returned to the Alexander Palace to spend their time there until the late autumn.

149. Alexander Palace. 1792–96, architect: G. Quarenghi

150. Alexander Palace. Corner Drawing Room of the Empress Alexandra Fiodorovna

151. Alexander Palace. Nicholas II's New Study

150

152

153

Nicholas I had some rooms and the park redesigned in the then fashionable Romantic manner. Later Emperor Alexander III had his apartments in the right-hand wing of the palace.

The palace interiors suffered during the war. In the summer of 1997, a permanent exhibition was opened in the left wing of the building. Today, certain elements of the Reception Room, Nicholas II's New Study and Alexandra Fiodorovna's Corner Drawing Room have been recreated and provide a fascinating backdrop to the exhibitions of historical costumes, weapons and objects of applied art to be found within their walls. In Nicholas II's beautifully preserved Study, where the working environment of the last Russian Emperor has been recreated, hangs a portrait of Nicholas II's father painted by the great Russian artist, Valentin Serov. In the children's quarters, visitors can see dresses once worn by the grand princesses and outfits and toys belonging to the Tsarevich Alexei.

In 1910–12 Vladimir Pokrovsky and Stepan Krichinsky erected for Nicholas II near the Alexander Palace the Cathedral of the Fiodorovskaya Icon of the Mother of God which became the focal

155

152. V. Makovsky. *Portrait of Nicholas II*

153. N. Bodarevsky. *Empress Alexandra Fiodorovna*. 1907

154. Nicholas II's Study in the Alexander Palace. 1920s. Photograph

155. Anonymous artist. *Portrait of Tsarevich Alexis*. 1910

156. Emperor Nicholas II and his family. 1904. Photograph

157. The Lilac Study of the Empress in the Alexander Palace. 1920s. Photograph

156

154

157

centre of the closed royal town. Its architecture reproduced the imagery and decorative motifs of ancient Russian Orthodox churches.

The Chinoiserie style found its embodiment at Tsarskoye Selo in a number of bridges in the Catherine Park and, in particular, in the ensemble known as the Chinese Village put up on the orders of Catherine the Great at the border of the Catherine and Alexander Parks. The latter comprises ten houses with intricate lines and decorative curved roofs. In the late nineteenth century the interior design of the cottages was changed to house the guests of the imperial family. Every pavillion was furnished with a bed, a small table, a wardrobe, a chest of drawers, a writing desk. It was equipped with

158. Alexander Park. Large Chinese Bridge. 1780s, architect: Ch. Cameron

159. Alexander Park. Dragon Bridge. 1785, architect: Ch. Cameron

160. Alexander Park. Creaking Pavilion. 1778–86, architect: Yu. Velten

161

162

tea- and coffee services (samovar included). Every cottage overlooked a small garden.

Situated in the Alexander Park, this complex is linked to the Catherine Park by two bridges. One of these is the Great Caprice, which constitutes a unique work of park architecture. The bridge is crowned with an elegant pagoda in which the European form of the octagonal rotunda is combined with an Eastern-style upturned roof. The second is the Cross Bridge, a fascinating structure consisting of two intersecting spans. On the bridge itself stands an octagonal pavilion with a curved roof, which sports an ornamental spike topped with a sphere.

The Creaking Pavilion was erected nearby to the design of Yury Velten. This pavilion crowned with weather-vanes attracted visitors' attention primarily by its unusual chinoiserie decoration.

A complex of "Chinese amusements" was increased by the construction of a group of the so-called

161. Alexander Park. Small Chinese Bridge. 1781–82, architect: Ch. Cameron

162, 165. Alexander Park. Chinese Village. 1782–98, architects: A. Rinaldi, V. Neyelov and Ch. Cameron; 1817–22, architect: V. Stasov

163. Alexander Park. Cross Bridge. 1776–79, architects: V. and I. Neyelov

164. Alexander Park. Great Caprice. 1772–74, architect: V. Neyelov

166

166. Alexander Park. Chinese Bridge. 1784, architect: Ch. Cameron

167. Alexander Park. View of the Cross Canal

168. Alexander Park.
Arsenal. 1816–34, architect: A. Menelaws

169. Alexander Park. Chapel Tower. 1825–28, architect: A. Menelaws
→
170. View of the Catherine Palace

Chinese Bridges created in the late 1770s and early 1780s. Besides the Cross Bridge, there are four of them — the Dragon Bridge, two iron Chinese bridges and the Large Stone Bridge.

The architectural wonders of Tsarskoye Selo are not only to be seen in the grounds of the parks, but also in the town. On the road that runs alongside the Alexander Park, the Egyptian Gates, designed by Menelaws, were erected in 1827–30. The gateposts that flank the arch resemble truncated pyramids. They are decorated with rows of reliefs showing genuine Egyptian characters. The stylised stems of the sacred Egyptian flower, the lotus, are entwined in the metal grille. These gates formed the main entrance to the town from the Petersburg side.

168

169

ЦАРСКОЕ СЕЛО

Альбом на английском языке

Издательство «П-2»

Производитель – ЗАО «П-2»
192029, Россия, Санкт-Петербург, пр. Обуховской Обороны, д. 95, корп. 2